Nerja
Travel Guide

Quick Trips Series

Table of Contents

NERJA & COSTA DEL SOL (EAST)   6

🌐 CUSTOMS & CULTURE 8

🌐 GEOGRAPHY..10

🌐 WEATHER & BEST TIME TO VISIT 11

SIGHTS & ACTIVITIES: WHAT TO SEE & DO   14

🌐 NERJA CAVES 14

🌐 BALCON DE EUROPA 17

🌐 EL SALVADOR CHURCH 19

🌐 LA ERMITA DE NUESTRA SENORA DE LAS ANGUSTIAS 21

🌐 EL AGUILA AQUEDUCT 22

🌐 BURRIANA BEACH 23

🌐 FRIGILIANA VILLAGE 25

🌐 NERJA DONKEY SANCTUARY 26

🌐 MARO VILLAGE 28

🌐 THE ALHAMBRA (GRANADA) 29

🌐 ALBAYZIN NEIGHBORHOOD (GRANADA)............................35

🌐 CATHEDRAL OF GRANADA 37

BUDGET TIPS   41

🌐 ACCOMMODATION 41

Hostal Alhambra..41

Hotel Bajamar...42

Villa Flamenca..43

Hotel Perla Marina..43

Hotel Plaza Cavana...44

Hostal Veronica..45

🌐 RESTAURANTS, CAFÉS & BARS 46

Marisqueria La Marina 46

La Puntilla...47

El Pulguilla 48

Merendero Ayo 48

Moreno..49

El Aji..50

🌐 SHOPPING 50

Nerja's Open Market 50

Nerja Book Centre 51

Alcaiciera..51

Artespana 52

Caldereria Nueva Street 52

KNOW BEFORE YOU GO   54

🌐 ENTRY REQUIREMENTS 54

🌐 HEALTH INSURANCE......................................54

🌐 TRAVELLING WITH PETS.................................55

🌐 AIRPORTS...56

🌐 AIRLINES...57

🌐 CURRENCY...58

🌐 BANKING & ATMS 58

🌐 CREDIT CARDS 58

🌐 TOURIST TAXES 59

🌐 RECLAIMING VAT 59

🌐 TIPPING POLICY...60

🌐 MOBILE PHONES 61

🌐 DIALLING CODE 62

🌐 EMERGENCY NUMBERS 62

🌐 PUBLIC HOLIDAYS 62

🌐 TIME ZONE 63

🌐 DAYLIGHT SAVINGS TIME 64

🌐 SCHOOL HOLIDAYS 64

🌐 TRADING HOURS 64

🌐 DRIVING LAWS 65

🌐 DRINKING LAWS..65

🌐 SMOKING LAWS 66

🌐 ELECTRICITY...66

🌐 FOOD & DRINK 67

Nerja & Costa del Sol (East)

Tourists are increasingly discovering the eastern Costa del Sol on the coast of Spain's Axarquía province. Here the cliffs meet the Mediterranean Sea and the charming seaside resort of Nerja is nestled in the foothills of the dramatic Sierra Almijara.

NERJA & COSTA DEL SOL (EAST) TRAVEL GUIDE

With whiffs of traditional Moorish influence and a historic devotion to fishing, Nerja is a much-loved holiday location for those looking to meet the more peaceful face of the Costa del Sol.

Formerly known as *Detunda* in Roman times, the city of Nerja was later named *Narixa* by the Moors, meaning "abundant springs"; a fit name for this jewel of a seaside resort. Its history dates back to about 30,000 years ago, a fact evident by the Paleolithic remains uncovered in the caves present in region.

With no high-rise hotel buildings in sight and strict architectural planning regulations in place, Nerja is all about its narrow and winding cobbled streets, balconies brimming with geraniums, whitewashed artsy local stores and Tapas bars. It is also the proud home of the Nerja

Caves (*Cuevas de Nerja*), discovered in 1959 and currently the 3rd most visited monument in Spain as well as the famous 9th century Balcon de Europa – a favorite meeting place and viewpoint among tourists due to its stunning panoramic sights of the Mediterranean sea.

Nerja also boasts about 13 kilometers of a variety of beaches; from crowded to isolated, from urbanized to wild, some equipped and some largely untouched. Some of the region's beaches are internationally renowned and awarded, case in point being the popular Burriana, a Blue Flag beach where the availability of facilities will delight any water sports' fan.

Stepping out of the city limits, you can't help but feel drawn to multiple nearby locations worth visiting; from the white labyrinth-like Andalucian village of Frigiliana just a few miles inland to the very accessible city of Granada - home of the world renowned Alhambra, the charm of the Costa del Sol Oriental is infinite.

🌏 Customs & Culture

The seaside city of Nerja now has a population of over 22,000 which is a somewhat stark contrast to its history of a tranquil and sleepy fishing village. Although its summer destination appeal as well as the foreign resident community has been on the steady rise, the local inhabitants and authorities are doing their best to retain the traditional culture and feel of the city therefore preserving its charm. It is this charm that makes Nerja a cherished location for Spaniards and foreigner travelers alike, as well as for the many artists and writers that have flocked to the region inspired by its dramatic landscape.

NERJA & COSTA DEL SOL (EAST) TRAVEL GUIDE

The proximity of the dramatic Nerja caves has made it a favorite location for many cultural events such as ballet and flamenco performances in the summer. World famous artists such as Jose Carreras and Montserrat Caballe have performed inside the caves which offer a unique stage and special acoustics.

The local *Nerjenos* take their heritage and traditions quite seriously and are devoted to the frequent festivities (such as the San Isidro, San Juan and Virgen del Carmen) which are a vital part of the region's culture. With a festival scheduled during almost each month of the year, Nerja gives visitors what many other resorts fail to provide: the opportunity to participate in the local culture, feel welcome and create meaningful memories.

🌐 Geography

The Costa del Sol Oriental, the eastern part of the sunny Costa del Sol is made up of the coastal municipalities of the Axarquía province. These include (from west to east) the municipalities of Rincón de la Victoria, Vélez-Málaga, Algarrobo, Torrox and the easternmost Nerja. The town of Nerja has been constructed on a ledge some 100 feet above sea level, giving it magnificent views of the surrounding area.

Narja's location is very convenient; only 50km away from Malaga and 100 km away from the historic Granada, both cities with international airports. But beyond the ease of getting into the city, the proximity of both larger cities makes Nerja a great base from which to explore the region. The trip from Malaga airport to Nerja takes around 40 minutes on the motorway.

Within Nerja, there are two local bus routes and the town is also connected via bus lines to many cities in the wider region, including Malaga, Granada, Cordoba, Seville and Almeria.

🌐 Weather & Best Time to Visit

The region boasts a mild climate which gives it a year-round travel appeal. It has been said that the Costa del Sol Oriental has the best climate from the whole of the Costa del Sol coast due to the protective effect of the high mountains jutting into the Mediterranean.

The coastline is thus shielded from cold north winds and enjoys a subtropical microclimate with more than 300 days of sunshine a year. The average summer temperatures are around 77° F while in winter they are about 59° F.

In winter, it is a preferred location for those wanting to escape the grim winter and bask in the sun; in the summer months it is brimming with visitors, celebrations and entertainment.

But the best time to visit Nerja and the surrounding region is definitely during spring or fall, when the crowds are minimal and you can have the city to yourself. Nevertheless, it is more than likely that once you visit Nerja you will want to return and soak it all up again, perhaps from a different seasonal perspective. It is this appeal of Nerja that has put it on the map as one of the most desired retirement locations in Europe.

Sights & Activities: What to See & Do

Nerja Caves

Cueva de Nerja, Maro, Nerja 29787

Tel: +34 952 529 520

http://www.thenerjacaves.com/

One of Spain's most treasured historical sites and an official National Monument, the spectacular Nerja Caves (*Cuevas de Nerja*) located just on the outside of Nerja's city limits, are actually a collection of caverns with combined length of almost five kilometres. The amazing initial discovery of the caves dates back to 1959 when five Maro village locals decided to investigate the mystery behind a large population of bats exiting through holes in rock formations blocked by stalactites. When they managed to enter into the caverns through a narrow sinkhole, they unearthed skeletons and ceramic pottery.

Soon enough, medical experts and photographers flocked

the location and the magnitude of the discovery was

widely documented. The Nerja Caves were inaugurated in

1960 and are currently the third most visited monument in

Spain.

Remains found in the caves have witnessed to the fact

that they were populated as far back as 25,000 BC and

up to the Bronze Age. It is believed that within a stretch of

4,000 years starting from 25,000 BC, the caves were

used by both humans and hyenas at certain times,

whereas after this period humans had settled in the

caverns permanently. Evidence found in and around the

caves also points to the conclusion that the cavern's

inhabitants, mostly devoted to hunting, used the

surrounding area for farming and pottery production.

Amazing discoveries, such as the world's largest stalagmite, with an imposing height of 32 meters, as well as cave paintings that may date back to the Neanderthal period have been found in the cavern. It has been speculated that the cave may hold the world's oldest artworks ever to be found, including six paintings of seals that may be at least 42,000 years old and may be the only known Neanderthal art to be discovered.

The cave is separated into two sections: Nerja I and Nerja II, each consisting of galleries and halls. The first section hosts the Show Gallery (open to the public) and is accessible by a flight of stairs ending at the Entrance Hall. Two more galleries (the Upper Gallery and the New Gallery, located in Nerja II), are only accessible during special group visits as these contain a large number of prehistoric paintings discovered in the caves.

One of the cavern's chambers is naturally shaped as an amphitheater and thus is a frequent venue for concerts. Each August, the Room of the Cascade, with its capacity of 600 seats and excellent acoustics, is the home of the Festival of Music and Dance.

Visitors should note that a moderate level of fitness is required due to the many stairs in the cavern. Neither wheelchairs nor pushchairs are allowed in the caves and flash photography is forbidden in most of the cave's areas.

The Nerja caves, 3 kilometres away from Nerja's center, are accessible by bus from Nerja and Malaga. A car park (costing 1 euro), a restaurant, a museum as well as a gift shop are all available at the premises. During the off-season (September – June), the caverns are open from 10:00-14:00 and 16:00-18:30 while during summertime their working hours are 10:00-14:00 and then 16:00-19:30. The entry fee for the caves is €8.5 for adults, €4.5 for children 6-12 years, and €4 for seniors and college groups.

🌐 Balcon de Europa

Paseo Balcón de Europa, Nerja 29780

Initially a 9th century castle and later the home of a fortified tower destroyed during the Peninsular Wars, the Balcony of Europe (*Balcon de Europa*) is nowadays Nerja's main viewpoint offering breathtaking sights of the Mediterranean which are certainly one of the best in the

Costa del Sol. The origin of its name is believed to be linked to King Alfonso XX of Spain who, while visiting Nerja after the 1884 earthquake, was mesmerized by the views and is said to have used the term "Balcony of Europe" to describe the location. The King's life-sized statue now stands by the railing, while two cannons act as reminders of its history as a fortress.

The Balcon de Europa is located on a rocky cliff and is undoubtedly the focal point of Nerja and also often used as the preferred setting for a wide range of events, including concerts and unforgettable New Year celebrations.

The fully pedestrianized palm tree lined Paseo Balcon de Europa promenade is flanked by many restaurants, bars and cafés as well as populated with a variety of street artists and performers. The nearby square Plaza Balcon de Europa is also frequented for its high quality bars and restaurants.

The Balcon de Europa provides excellent views of the Calahonda and La Caletilla beaches as well as access to the El Salon beach. Right at the Calahonda gap, at the beginning of the Paseo de Carabineros, a picturesque rocky path takes eager explorers down to the famous Burriana Beach.

🌐 El Salvador Church

Balcón de Europa, Nerja 29780

Just opposite the Balcon de Europa is the picturesque Church of El Salvador (*Iglesia El Salvador*), originally built in 1505, then further renovated and extended during the

17th (under the ministry of Alonso de Molina Duran) and 18th century. Its last restoration was done in 1997. The church has been built in a mix of baroque and Moorish style, commonly known as mudéjar.

Constructed on a three-naved cross and featuring a bell tower with an ornate 'Rosa' clock, the church is most notably known for the Grenadine frescoes found in its interior, made in the 18th century, as well as Francisco Hernandez' (local Axarquian painter) contemporary annunciation mural done in 1990. The façade is made in a Baroque style.

With a calm and serene air about it, the El Salvador is a very important part of the Nerja community and a quiet heaven in a central location. The church is a favorite place for weddings and in recent years it has also become a magnet for foreign couples who wish to be wedded in such a quaint setting. Weddings take place on Fridays, Saturdays and Sundays and travellers often cherish the opportunity to witness such an occasion.

🌐 La Ermita de Nuestra Senora de las Angustias

Plaza de la Ermita, Nerja 29780

A beautiful baroque style chapel, the *La Ermita Nuestra Senora de las Angustias* Chapel (Hermitage of Our Lady of Anguish) was built in 1720. Inside it, an exquisite 18th century Pentecost oil mural painted over the high neo-baroque altar has been attributed to an unknown Granada painter.

The church was founded by Bernarda Maria Alferez of the Granada-based Lopez de Alcantara family, in honor of the Virgen de las Angustias who is the patron saint of Nerja. The chapel was later handed over to the town of Nerja and the Cathedral of Malaga.

In close proximity of the chapel, one can visit the La Sala Mercado exhibition hall. A free car park, off the N-340, is within a short distance as well.

From Monday to Friday, the chapel's visiting hours are 8:00-14:00 and then 16:00-20:00 while during weekends it is only open to the general public during the mornings.

🌐 El Aguila Aqueduct

Barranco de la Coladilla de Cazadores, Nerja

Though it may look like it was built during Roman times, the *Acueducto del Aguila* (Eagle Aqueduct) is actually a contemporary engineering feat, completed towards the end of the 19th century in order to provide water to the old San Joaquin de Maro sugar factory.

The aqueduct's architect was Francisco Cantarero and the structure features four brick arcade floors with a total of 37 arches. The origin of the double-headed eagle shaped weather vane on the top of the spire has not been accurately established but is believed to be linked to the fact that eagles were nesting in the Maro hills during the time of construction. Currently the water is only being used for irrigating farmland around Nerja. A complete restoration was done on the aqueduct in 2011 and the Andalucian Government recognized it as a site of special cultural interest.

The region surrounding the aqueduct is known by the locals as "Cardiac Hill" and it is located off the A340 road leading from Nerja to Maro and about 30 minutes by foot from the center of Nerja. No timetable restrictions apply in regards to visiting hours as this is a public area.

🌐 Burriana Beach

Almost a standalone resort on its own, the 800 meter long Burriana Beach (*Playa Burriana*) is on the list of regular winners of the coveted "Blue Flag Beach" awards organized by the European Union as well as the "Q for Quality" flag awarded by Spanish authorities. It is the most popular beach in Nerja.

Amenities and services required by even the most demanding beach lovers (including sunbeds, paddle boats, beach volleyball nets, showers, lifeguards and play areas) are available at this beach where the sea gets deep quite quickly. The promenade Paseo Maritimo Antonio Mercero lines the back of the beach where one can find many Spanish restaurants and *Merenderos* (open air cafes), some with regular Flamenco shows in the summertime. It is here also that one can see the sculpture of a director's chair, homage to Antonio Mercero who produced the popular Spanish TV series *Verano Azul,* set in Nerja. A number of souvenir shops, bars, restaurants, a dive center and a supermarket can be found just behind the promenade.

The beach is accessed from two entrance points, both arriving through steep downhill paths or alternatively with a car or a taxi.

🌏 Frigiliana Village

Some seven kilometers from Nerja and positioned high in the Almijara, Tejea and Alhama mountains at an elevation of around 430 meters above sea level, the pretty village of Frigiliana is a regular attraction drawing visitors from the region. It has received many awards for its beauty and efforts in tradition and history conservation.

Considered one of the most picturesque typical white-washed Andalucian villages, it is a maze of narrow, winding, cobbled streets. Though walking through the village is by far the best way to experience it, visitors should note that some of the streets are steep. The true reward for the persistent explorer can be found in the numerous small shops, bars and restaurants seemingly hiding behind every corner.

The old historical center of the village has a definite Moorish air about it, complete with a plethora of colors from the flowers overflowing from balconies, windows and ledges. With a population of around 3,000, Frigiliana village is most definitely one of the must-sees in the Costa del Sol Oriental region. Select sights in the village include the 16th century Church of San Antonio, the Royal Granary, the Chapel of Ecce Home and of course the Mudejar District which is dotted with ceramic mosaics that provide an excellent narrative of the Moorish uprising in the region. Frigiliana is also famous for its local sweet wine known as *Vino de Frigiliana.*

The village of Frigiliana is an easy 10 minute drive from Nerja on the MA-105 road and is also connected to Nerja via bus.

⊙ Nerja Donkey Sanctuary

N-340, Nerja 29780

http://www.nerjadonkeysanctuary.com

A seemingly unlikely attraction near a popular coastal resort, the 2004-founded Nerja Donkey Sanctuary is in fact an English-run registered charity.

A favorite among the younger Nerja visitors, its main purpose is the rescue, care for and protection of donkeys, horses and mules. The sanctuary staff rescues abandoned and abused animals found in the region and has so far provided a home to hundreds of horses, mules and donkeys, some of which have been moved to new safer homes. The charity has also offered shelter for other animals such as goats, pigs, cats and sheep.

During winter, its opening hours are 10:00-16:00 on weekdays and 10:00-14:00 on weekends. In the summer, the sanctuary operates from 10:00-14:00 and then from 17:00-18:00 (17:00-20:00 in August). The sheltered animals are also available for a symbolic "adoption" which costs €20 per year. The entry to the sanctuary is free but visitors are advised to bring carrots and feed the donkeys. Volunteers are also welcome.

🌍 Maro Village

The charming village of Maro, only 3 kilometers east of Nerja, is actually located in the close proximity of the Nerja Caves and has a population of 800. The Maro Village is known for its Chestnut Fiesta, organized on the last day of October each year. This event gives the opportunity to visitors to immerse themselves in the culture of the locals when literally tons of chestnuts are eaten in an atmosphere of celebration along with plenty of music and dancing.

The village's history goes back to the early Christian era. The former *Detunda* (defence) was the first structure built in the village and is now the location of the Plaza de la Iglesia and the Casa Granade. A true Andalucian coastal village, it is specifically proud of one of its prettiest streets; the Calle Maravillas offers fascinating views of the sea. A highlight not to be missed is the parish church of Senora de las Maravillas.

Maro is still a relatively unspoilt village, even with the high quality restaurants and tapas bars with spectacular views. The village has a small beach set in a cove, accessible through a winding path down the cliffs, where snorkeling is highly recommended.

🌐 The Alhambra (Granada)

Calle Real de la Alhambra s/n, Granada 18009

Tel: 902 441 221, Reservations Tel: 902 888 001

http://www.alhambra-patronato.es/

A visit to the region would not be complete without at least a day spent in Granada, a mere hour away from Nerja, where the focal point of interest is undoubtedly the majestic Alhambra.

Nowadays a UNESCO World Heritage Site, the Alhambra was originally constructed as a fortress in 889. On the rocky hills by the banks of the River Darro, perfectly protected by mountains and covering an area of about 140,000m², it is a rather imposing reddish colored structure (which is the origin of the Alhambra's name meaning red castle – *qa'lat al-Hamra*) with no external hint of the beauty found in its interior. While its original purpose was that of a military area, it later became the chosen residence of royalty. When the Nasrid kingdom was established in the mid-13th century, the king Mohammed ibn Yusuf ben Nasr converted it to a royal palace, known as Alhamar.

In the three centuries that followed, the Alhambra became a citadel consisting of two main sections: the military area (*Alcazaba*) with the barracks of the royal guards and the court palace city (*Alcazar*) where the famous Nasrid Palaces were located – a central highlight of the Alhambra.

These include three interconnected palaces with impressive decorations and a curious mix of rooms, royal apartments, courtyards and fountains. This court section, known as the medina, is also the home of the Charles V

Palace, a Renaissance structure built by the Holy Roman

Emperor Charles V in 1527 and practically inserted within

the previous Nasrid fortifications.

The *Alcazaba* (citadel) was Alhambra's oldest section,

dating from the ninth century and only the imposing

external walls and towers remain nowadays. In 1492, as a

symbol of the Spanish conquest of Granada, the flag of

Ferdinand and Isabela was first raised here, on the

citadel's watchtower.

Most of the buildings found in the palaces are

quadrangular and all rooms open to a central court.

During the centuries, additions of new buildings were

done always following the quadrangular rule, though at

different scales. The Muslim rulers who worked on

extending the palace were also devoted to adding a number of column arcades, pools and running water fountains in the interior.

For many centuries, the Alhambra was a victim of neglect, only being rediscovered by travelers and experts in the 19th century. Restorations were in order and nowadays the Alhambra is one of Spain's main attractions and the most majestic sample of Spanish Arab-Islamic architecture. Lacking the notable Byzantine influences found in other Spanish regions' period structures, the Alhambra in Granada is a majestic pinnacle of Moorish art in Europe.

The Alhambra's garden, brimming with flowers, was planted with roses as well as orange and myrtle trees during Moorish times. A forest of English Elms, a dense population of nightingales as well as multiple cascades and fountains all adorn this majestic garden.

Opposite the Alhambra, one can find an independent palace surrounded by gardens and orchards which was the favorite leisure spot of the Granadine kings and is known as the Generalife. Many viewpoints, pavilions and patios as well as pools make any visitor understand why the sultans also preferred the Generalife as a summer retreat.

One can access the Alhambra Park from the city of Granada via the Gate of Pomegranates (*Puerta de las Granadas*), at the fountain and on to *the Puerta de la Justicia* (Gate of Judgement) which is Alhambra's main entrance. Five car parks are available by the Alhambra where parking costs approximately €3.5/hr.

NERJA & COSTA DEL SOL (EAST) TRAVEL GUIDE

The city authorities at Granada are strict with the limitations of daily visitors to the Alhambra, with only 6,600 people allowed to enter each day. Opening hours are 08:30-20:00 from mid-March to mid-October and 8:30-18:00 in the winter months. Night visits are also available from Tuesday to Saturday from 22:00-23:30 during the summer. The general entrance fee is €13; a reduced fee of €9 applies. Children up to 11 years are admitted free while those 12-15 years are charged €8.

About two thirds of the available tickets can be bought up to three months in advance through the Caixa bank's ticketmaster online (http://www.alhambra-tickets.es) and printed out from the entrance or one of the Caixa machines in Granada.

Only about a third of the visit tickets are indeed available on the day of the visit through the ticket office at the Alhambra resulting in long queues. Visitors wanting to purchase tickets on the spot are advised to arrive before the ticket office opens at 8:00. Another way to bypass the queues is to head to the automated machines that allow visitors to purchase tickets with a pin-operated debit or credit card. Only a few sections of the Alhambra are accessible without tickets and these include the courtyard of the Palace of Charles V, the church, the bathhouse and the craft shops.

Purchased tickets indicate the visitor's allocated time to visit the Nasrid palaces and advance purchases provide the option of selecting the half-hour slot dedicated to this section. The Alhambra, with its 3.5km long route around its premises, can easily become a half-day visit for those wanting to see everything.

◉ Albayzin Neighborhood (Granada)

The Albayzin quarter, a sleepy and cozy part of Granada, is a contrast to the rest of the city's busy atmosphere. This original Arab neighborhood rises on a hill and is linked to the rest of the city with the long Plaza Nueva. Much like the Alhambra, the Albayzin neighborhood is UNESCO-listed with many of its historical buildings carefully restored.

Some of the buildings, including the archeological museum of Casa de Castril and the cultural center at Casa de Porras (initially a 16th century Mudejar mansion) are open to the public. Any visitor is undoubtedly to be captivated by the labyrinth of white houses, churches, palaces and the lovely carmenes (essentially villas with enclosed gardens), all decorated by vegetation.

The neighborhood serves as a picturesque witness to the successful blending of Moorish and Andalucian residential architecture. Most of its significance is linked to the quarter's plan of narrow winding streets and tiny squares. Excavations in the region have proven that the hill where the Albayzin is located was occupied as early as Roman times. During the 8th century, the governor Asap ben Abderrahman built a fortress on the spot where today's Plaza de San Nicolas can be found.

Granada flourished during the Nasrid dynasty's rule as it was the last standing foothold of the Arabs in the Iberian

Peninsula. It was then that the Albayzin become the home of many craftsmen and traders. After the Reconquista in 1492, Albayzin's population stood at almost 60,000 with the settlement of a sizable Christian population following the emigration of the Muslims. The Moorish-influenced neighborhood was left somewhat untouched however; later structures and decorations were blended into the existing ones. The lower part of the neighborhood is the home of many gift shops and tea rooms where explorers will appreciate a cup of aromatic tea coupled with a delightful Arab sweet.

With the fascinating bohemian atmosphere of a town within a town, the Albayzin neighborhood also provides spectacular views of the Alhambra and the Sierra Nevada, particularly from the San Nicolas church viewpoint at sunset. To witness the best panoramic views of the city of Granada, head to the San Cristobal viewpoint.

The Albayzin neighborhood is accessible via bus number 31 from Plaza Nueva in Granada. Visitors are advised that navigating around the neighborhood is best done on foot as cars cannot effectively circulate through the maze of narrow streets.

Cathedral of Granada

Ran Via de Colon 5, Granada 18001

Tel: +34 958 222 959

http://www.catedraldegranada.com/

Construction of the Granada Cathedral was commissioned by Queen Isabela immediately after the Reconquista in 1492 and work started in 1523. Initially the cathedral was planned in the Gothic style but as the construction happened during the Spanish Renaissance time, the influence of that time period can be observed.

The architect Enrique Egas laid the Gothic foundations from 1518 to 1523 on top of what was the city's main mosque in Moorish times. Egas was replaced by the Renaissance pioneer Diego de Siloe who worked on the cathedral for almost 40 years. Other architects followed, frequently altering the initial plans. It took a total of 181 years for the cathedral to be fully constructed in 1704 and it is still considered incomplete by many as the two large towers initially planned for were never completely built; only one of them was added but with a lower height than initially designed.

Busts of Adam and Eve and effigies of King Ferdinand and Queen Isabela can be found in the main chapel, while the Chapel of the Trinity features paintings by El Greco, Jusepe de Ribera and Alonso Cano. The burial chamber holds the tombs of Catholic kings. The Cathedral is quite large with a length of 115 meters and width of 67 meters and its interior if of golden hues with plenty of light.

The Granada Cathedral is next to the Capilla Real (Royal Chapel) which can be entered separately. The Capilla was constructed in the Plateresque style and is the burial home of Queen Isabela and King Ferdinand.

The ticket for a general admission costs €4 and entry is free for children under 10 and people with disabilities. Student groups qualify for discounts but must contact the Cathedral in advance. The Cathedral is open Monday to

Saturday from 10:45-13:30 and from 16:00-19:00 in winter

months, and only in the afternoon hours on public

holidays and Sundays. From April 1st to October 31st one

can visit the Cathedral from 10:45-13:30 and 16:00-20:00

on weekdays and Saturdays and only during the

afternoons on Sundays and public holidays.

Budget Tips

 # Accommodation

Hostal Alhambra

Calle Antonio Millón 12, Nerja 29780

Tel: +34 952 522 174

http://www.hostalalhambra.es/alhambra-nerja.php

Only 300 meters from Torrecila Beach and a five minute walk from the Balcon de Europa, the Alhambra guesthouse features soundproofed pastel colored rooms, some with a balcony or terrace. The location is within close proximity to a number of bars, restaurants and shops while the El Salvador church is a mere 5 minute walk away.

Prices for a double room accommodation in this 15 room guesthouse start at a very affordable €50, making it particularly attractive to budget travellers.

Hotel Bajamar

Calle Castilla Perez 4, Nerja

Tel: +34 952 523 204

http://www.hotelbajamar.com/

In the heart of Nerja and in proximity to its wonderful beaches, the typically white Andalucian Hotel Bajamar is one of the best choices for families and leisure visitors due to its location. A rooftop swimming pool offers exquisite views of both the Mediterranean and the mountains while a bar, 24 hour reception desk, Wi-Fi Internet and free parking for guests are also available. The hotel is located at a 600 meter distance from the El

Salon beach and a 10 minute walk from the Balcon de Europa.

Single rooms in the low season start at €35 per night while larger family rooms in the high season cost around €100 per night.

Villa Flamenca

C/ de Andalucía 1, Nerja 29780

Tel: +34 952 523 200

http://www.hotelvillaflamenca.es/

Only 400 meters from Nerja beach, the Villa Flamenca provides air conditioned rooms equipped with satellite TV and free Wi-Fi as well as a pool.

At a 15 minute walk from the focal Balcon de Europa, the hotel features 126 rooms and prices for a twin room accommodation with breakfast begin at about €70 in the high season, though early booking offers available upon consultation with the hotel may provide attractive discounts.

Hotel Perla Marina

Calle Mérida 7, Nerja 29780

Tel: +34 952 523 350

http://www.hotelperlamarina.com

Right on Nerja's seafront, the four-star 198 room Hotel Perla Marina provides majestic sea views and features two pools and a café. The hotel includes a spa facility and a restaurant serving Mediterranean food. A café set on a seaside terrace is also highly appreciated among visitors as is the proximity to the Balcon de Europa, only a 15 minute walk away.

The price for a double room with breakfast in the high season starts at €90 per night, with half board options available as well.

Hotel Plaza Cavana

Plaza Cavana 10, Nerja 29780

Tel: +34 952 524 000

http://www.hotelplazacavana.com/

The Hotel Plaza Cavana boasts an excellent location at only 100 meters from the beach and the popular Balcon de Europa. Two swimming pools, one of which situated on the rooftop, are available. Rooms are spacious, all with a TV, safe and air-conditioning. The premises also include a café bar, a poolside snack bar, a restaurant and a gym.

The Plaza Cavana was expanded in 2004 and now features a total of 39 rooms and the price for a double room in the high season starts at a little over €100.

Hostal Veronica

Angel 15-17, Granada 18002

Tel: +34 958 258 145

http://www.hostalveronica.com/

If you are visiting multiple attractions in Granada, it may be worth planning an overnight stay in this Andalucian city. At a distance of only 500 meters from the Granada Cathedral, the Hostal Veronica is right in the center. The air-conditioned rooms with TV are simple but some feature the typical Andalucian original ceramic floor tiles.

Rooms all come with small balconies and private

bathrooms and prices for a double room start at very

affordable €30.

🌍 Restaurants, Cafés & Bars

Marisqueria La Marina

Calle Castilla Pérez 28, Nerja 29780

Tel: +34 952 521 299

The Marisqueria La Marina on the Plaza de la Marina at

the west of Nerja is an informal seafood tapas bar with

most of its table outside. Each drink ordered at the bar

comes with a free tapa of seafood salad. Though it is a

rather no-frills place, it is perennially popular with the

locals.

Small fried fish typical of the coastal region as well as a large variety of shellfish and mollusks are all on the menu. The price for a beer and a tapa starts at €1.20. A daily menu (*menu del dia*) costs €8.5 and includes an appetizer, main dish, dessert and a drink.

La Puntilla

Bolivia 1, Nerja 29780

Tel: +34 952 528 951

A great value for money, the La Puntilla tapas bar offers Spanish seafood with a terrific variety of fresh fish and shellfish.

Though its location is not exactly on the seaside, it is a little gem of a restaurant well worth the trip. The fact that it is popular with the locals speaks to the quality of the food and wine served.

Fresh seafood dishes start at €4.00 with the locally famous gambas pil-pil (prawns in garlic and chilli) costin about €6.50 and a bottle of excellent Ribera wine about €24.00.

El Pulguilla

Calle Almirante Fernandez 26, Nerja 29780

Tel: +34 952 521 384

http://www.elpulguilla.com/bar-res.html

A typical Spanish fish and seafood restaurant, the El Pulguilla caters to a mostly Spanish target market due to the cheap drinks, free tapas and excellent seafood. On the large open air terrace, each drink comes with a free tapa dish while a bottle of wine comes with free 5 tapas, a fact appreciated by budget travellers. A prawn cocktail costs €6, marinated anchovies start at €5 while sautéed clams will set you back €9.

Merendero Ayo

Playa Burriana s/n, Nerja 29780

Tel: +34 952 522 289

http://www.ayonerja.com/

A no-frills restaurant right on Burriana beach, Ayo serves all-you-can-eat paella in a simple setting with plastic chairs and tables and has existed for over 30 year. It is a remarkable experience to watch the internationally known huge paella over the wood fire on a scenic beachfront setting on Burriana, surrounded by palm trees.

At €6.50 for a paella, it sure is a good value lunch choice at the beach. To add to its attraction, it should be noted that the owner, Francisco Ortega Ollala (known as "Ayo") is a legendary character in Nerja as he is one of the first locals to have discovered and entered the Nerja Caves in 1959.

Moreno

Lugar Playa Burriana s/n, Nerja 29780

Tel: +34 952 52 54 80

Another restaurant located on Burriana beach, the *merendero* Moreno is known for offering a free grappa at the end of every meal. The restaurant serves barbeque and seafood, all prepared on the open terrace with sea views.

El Aji

Plaza San Miguel Bajo 9, Granada 29780

Tel: +34 958 292 930

http://www.restauranteelaji.com/aji.html

When exploring the Albayzin quarter in Granada, make sure you find your way to the El Aji restaurant set on a scenic square. The menu is mostly traditional with a bit of a contemporary twist (such as prawns with tequila and honey). A quality bottle of wine costs about €13.

🌐 Shopping

Nerja's Open Market

Held every Tuesday and Sunday mornings, Nerja's street market opens around 9:00 and is the beloved pastime of travellers visiting the town on these days. It is a typical

Spanish market with fresh produce, breads, meat and fish, though one can also find stalls with clothing and accessories in the market and the sellers are always ready for bargaining. This is mostly so during the Sunday market, which is more of a flea market, so one can always count on uncovering something unique.

Nerja Book Centre

Calle Granada 32, Nerja 29780

http://www.nerjabookcentre.com/

The Nerja Book Centre in Nerja is a second-hand bookshop with a vast selection of books (over 30,000 in 15 different languages). Prices start at €0.90 per book and many rare first editions and out of print books can be discovered in this well stocked store.

Alcaiciera

Granada 29780

The Alcaiciera is a district rather than a singular shop; the name of the neighbourhood translates to House of Ceasar and dates back to Moorish times as this was the place where the Moors would sell silk. It is a popular area dotted with many souvenir shops as well as stores selling anything from t-shirts to fireworks. One is likely to find interesting wall hangings or rugs in this area.

Artespana

Realejo, Granada 29780

A government-run collective of artistic craftsman, the Artespaña used to be a market square in Moorish times. Nowadays it is the point of sale of various *Grenadino* crafts such as leather goods, textiles and brass and copperware.

Caldereria Nueva Street

La Calle Caldereria Nueva, Granada 29780

This is in fact a narrow street starting from the Plaza Nueva in the Albayzin district and is the home of many small gift shops and street stalls. One can definitely make a comparison to a Moroccan street market as a mish-mash of ceramics, lamps, clothing, jewellery, spices and other random products are being sold on the streets, often displayed on rugs on the pavement.

Know Before You Go

Entry Requirements

By virtue of the Schengen agreement, visitors from other countries in the European Union will not need a visa when visiting Spain. Additionally visitors from Switzerland, Norway, Lichtenstein, Iceland, Canada, the United Kingdom, Australia and the USA are also exempt. Independently travelling minors will need to carry written permission from their parents. If visiting from a country where you require a visa to enter Spain, you will also need to state the purpose of your visit and provide proof that you have financial means to support yourself for the duration of your stay. Unless you are an EU national, your passport should be valid for at least 3 months after the end of your stay.

Health Insurance

Citizens of other EU countries are covered for emergency health care in Spain. UK residents, as well as visitors from Switzerland are covered by the European Health Insurance Card (EHIC), which can be applied for free of charge. Visitors from non-Schengen countries will need to show proof of private health insurance that is valid for the duration of their stay in Spain, as part of their visa application.

🌍 Travelling with Pets

Spain participates in the Pet Travel Scheme (PETS) which allows UK residents to travel with their pets without requiring quarantine upon re-entry. Certain conditions will need to be met. The animal will have to be microchipped and up to date on rabies vaccinations. Additionally, you will need a PETS re-entry certificate issued by a UK vet, an Export Health Certificate (this is required by the Spanish authorities), an official Certificate of Treatment against dangerous parasites such as tapeworm and ticks and an official Declaration that your pet has not left the qualifying countries within this period. Pets from the USA or Canada may be brought in under the conditions of a non-commercial import. For this, your pet will also need to be microchipped (or marked with an identifying tattoo) and up to date on rabies vaccinations.

🌍 Airports

Adolfo Suárez Madrid–Barajas Airport (MAD) is the largest and busiest airport in Spain. It is located about 9km from the financial district of Madrid, the capital. The busiest route is the so-called "Puente Aéreo" or "air bridge", which connects Madrid with Barcelona. The second busiest airport in Spain is **Barcelona–El Prat Airport** (BCN), located about 14km southwest from the center of Barcelona. There are two terminals. The newer Terminal 1 handles the bulk of its traffic, while the older Terminal 2 is used by budget airlines such as EasyJet.

Palma de Mallorca Airport (PMI) is the third largest airport in Spain and one of its busiest in the summer time. It has the capacity of processing 25 million passengers annually. **Gran Canaria Airport** (LPA) handles around 10 million passengers annually and connects travellers with the Canary Islands. **Pablo Ruiz Picasso Malaga Airport** (AGP) provides access to the Costa del Sol. Other southern airports are **Seville Airport** (SVQ), **Jaen Federico Garcia Lorca Airport** (GRX) near Granada, **Jerez de la Frontera Airport**, which connects travellers to Costa del Luz and Cadiz and **Almeria Airport** (LEI).

🌐 Airlines

Iberia is the flag carrying national airline of Spain. Since a merger in 2010 with British Airways, it is part of the International Airlines Group (IAG). Iberia is in partnership with the regional carrier Air Nostrum and Iberia Express, which focusses on medium and short haul routes. Vueling is a low-cost Spanish airline with connections to over 100 destinations. In partnership with MTV, it also provides a seasonal connection to Ibiza. Volotea is a budget airline based in Barcelona, which mainly flies to European destinations. Air Europe, the third largest airline after Iberia and Vueling connects Europe to resorts in the Canaries and the Balearic Islands and also flies to North and South America. Swiftair flies mainly to destinations in Europe, North Africa and the Middle East.

Barcelona-El Prat Airport serves as a primary hub for Iberia Regional. It is also a hub for Vueling. Additionally it functions as a regional hub for Ryanair. Air Europe's primary hubs are at Palma de Mallorca Airport and Madrid Barajas Airport, but other bases are at Barcelona Airport and Tenerife South Airport. Air Nostrum is served by hubs at Barcelona Airport, Madrid Barajas Airport and Valencia Airport. Gran Canaria Airport is the hub for the regional airline, Binter Canarias.

🌍 Currency

Spain's currency is the Euro. It is issued in notes in denominations of €500, €200, €100, €50, €20, €10 and €5. Coins are issued in denominations of €2, €1, 50c, 20c, 10c, 5c, 2c and 1c.

🌍 Banking & ATMs

You should have no trouble making withdrawals in Spain if your ATM card is compatible with the MasterCard/Cirrus or Visa/Plus networks. If you want to save money, avoid using the dynamic currency conversion (DCC) system, which promises to charge you in your own currency for the Euros you withdraw. The fine print is that your rate will be less favorable. Whenever possible, opt to conduct your transaction in Euros instead. Do remember to advise your bank or credit card company of your travel plans before leaving.

🌍 Credit Cards

Visa and MasterCard will be accepted at most outlets that handle credit cards in Spain, but you may find that your American Express card is not as welcome at all establishments. While shops may still be able to accept transactions with older magnetic strip cards, you will need a PIN enabled card for transactions at automatic vendors such as ticket sellers. Do not be offended when asked to show proof of ID when paying by credit card. It is common practice in Spain and Spaniards are required by law to carry identification on them at all times.

🌍 Tourist Taxes

In the region of Catalonia, which includes Barcelona, a tourist tax of between €0.45 and €2.50 per night is levied for the first seven days of your stay. The amount depends on the standard of the establishment, but includes youth hostels, campgrounds, holiday apartments and cruise ships with a stay that exceeds 12 hours.

🌍 Reclaiming VAT

If you are not from the European Union, you can claim back VAT (or Value Added Tax) paid on your purchases in Spain. The VAT rate in Spain is 18 percent. VAT refunds are made on purchases of €90.15 and over from a single shop. Look for shops displaying Global Blue Tax Free Shopping signage. You will be required to fill in a form at the shop, which must then be stamped at the Customs office at the airport. Customs officers will want to inspect your purchases to make sure that they are sealed and unused. Once this is done, you will be able to claim your refund from the Refund Office at the airport. Alternately, you can mail the form to Global Blue once you get home for a refund on your credit card.

🌍 Tipping policy

In general, Spain does not really have much of a tipping culture and the Spanish are not huge tippers themselves. When in a restaurant, check your bill to see whether a gratuity is already included. If not, the acceptable amount will depend on the size of the meal, the prestige of the restaurant and the time of day. For a quick coffee, you can simply round the amount off. For lunch in a modest establishment, opt for 5 percent or one euro per person. The recommended tip for dinner would be more generous, usually somewhere between 7 and 10 percent. This will depend on the type of establishment.

In hotels, if there is someone to help you with your luggage, a tip of 1 euro should be sufficient. At railway stations and airports, a tip is not really expected. Rounding off the amount of the fare to the nearest euro would be sufficient for a taxi driver. If you recruited a private driver, you may wish to tip that person at the end of your association with him.

🌍 Mobile Phones

Most EU countries, including Spain uses the GSM mobile service. This means that most UK phones and some US and Canadian phones and mobile devices will work in Spain. While you could check with your service provider about coverage before you leave, using your own service in roaming mode will involve additional costs. The alternative is to purchase a Spanish SIM card to use during your stay in Spain.

Spain has four mobile networks. They are Movistar, Vodafone, Orange and Yoiga. Buying a Spanish SIM card is relatively simple and inexpensive. By law, you will be required to show some form of identification such as a passport. A basic SIM card from Vodafone costs €5. There are two tourist packages available for €15, which offers a combination of 1Gb data, together with local and international call time. Alternately, a data only package can also be bought for €15. From Orange, you can get a SIM card for free, with a minimum top-up purchase of €10. A tourist SIM with a combination of data and voice calls can be bought for €15. Movistar offers a start-up deal of €10. At their sub-branches, Tuenti, you can also get a free SIM, but the catch is that you need to choose a package to get it. The start-up cost at Yoiga is €20.

Dialling Code

The international dialling code for Spain is +34.

Emergency Numbers

All Emergencies: 112 (no area code required)

Police (municipal): 092

Police (national): 091

Police (tourist police, Madrid): 91 548 85 37

Police (tourist police, Barcelona): 93 290 33 27

Ambulance: 061 or 112

Fire: 080 or 112

Traffic: 900 123 505

Electricity: 900 248 248

Immigration: 900 150 000

MasterCard: 900 958 973

Visa: 900 99 1124

🌍 Public Holidays

1 January: New Year's Day (Año Nuevo)

6 January: Day of the Epiphany/Three Kings Day (Reyes Mago)

March/April: Good Friday

1 May: Labor Day (Día del Trabajo)

15 August: Assumption of Mary (Asunción de la Virgen)

12 October: National Day of Spain/Columbus Day (Fiesta Nacional de España or Día de la Hispanidad)

1 November: All Saints Day (Fiesta de Todos los Santos)

6 December: Spanish Constitution Day (Día de la Constitución)

8 December: Immaculate Conception (La Immaculada)

25 December: Christmas (Navidad)

Easter Monday is celebrated in the Basque region, Castile-La Mancha, Catalonia, La Rioja, Navarra and Valencia. 26

December is celebrated as Saint Stephen's Day in Catalonia and the Balearic Islands.

🌐 Time Zone

Spain falls in the Central European Time Zone. This can be calculated as Greenwich Mean Time/Co-ordinated Universal Time (GMT/UTC) +2; Eastern Standard Time (North America) -6; Pacific Standard Time (North America) -9.

🌐 Daylight Savings Time

Clocks are set forward one hour on the last Sunday in March and set back one hour on the last Sunday in October for Daylight Savings Time.

🌐 School Holidays

Spain's academic year is from mid-September to mid-June. It is divided into three terms with two short breaks of about two weeks around Christmas and Easter.

🌐 Trading Hours

Trading hours in Spain usually run from 9.30am to 1.30pm and from 4.30pm to 8pm, from Mondays to Saturdays. Malls and shopping centers often trade from 10am to 9pm without closing. During the peak holiday seasons, shops could stay open until 10pm. Lunch is usually served between 1pm and 3.30pm while dinner is served from 8.30 to 11pm.

🌐 Driving Laws

The Spanish drive on the right hand side of the road. You will need a driver's licence which is valid in the EC to be able to hire a car in Spain. The legal driving age is 18, but most rental companies will require you to be at least 21 to be able to rent a car. You will need to carry your insurance documentation and rental contract with you at all times, when driving. The speed limit in Spain is 120km per hour on motorways, 100km per hour on dual carriageways and 90km per hour on single carriageways. Bear in mind that it is illegal to drive in Spain wearing sandals or flip-flops.

You may drive a non-Spanish vehicle in Spain provided that it is considered roadworthy in the country where it is registered. As a UK resident, you will be able to drive a vehicle registered in the UK in Spain for up to six months, provided that your liabilities as a UK motorist, such as MOT, road tax and insurance are up to date for the entire period of your stay. The legal limit in Spain is 0.05, but for new drivers who have had their licence for less than two years, it is 0.03.

🌐 Drinking Laws

In Spain, the minimum drinking age is 18. Drinking in public places is forbidden and can be punished with a spot fine. In areas where binge drinking can be a problem, alcohol trading hours are often limited.

🌐 Smoking Laws

In the beginning of 2006, Spain implemented a policy banning smoking from all public and private work places. This includes schools, libraries, museums, stadiums, hospitals, cinemas, theatres and shopping centers as well as public transport. From 2011, smoking was also banned in restaurants and bars, although designated smoking areas can be created provided they are enclosed and well ventilated. Additionally tobacco products may only be sold from tobacconists and bars and restaurants where smoking is permitted. Smoking near children's parks, schools or health centers carries a €600 fine.

🌐 Electricity

Electricity: 220 volts

Frequency: 50 Hz

Your electrical appliances from the UK and Ireland should be able to function sufficiently in Spain, but since Spain uses 2 pin sockets, you will need a C/F adapter to convert the plug from 3 to 2-pins. The voltage and frequency is compatible with UK appliances. If travelling from the USA, you will need a converter or step-down transformer to convert your appliances to 110 volts. The latest models of many laptops, camcorders, cell phones and digital cameras are dual-voltage with a built in converter.

🌐 Food & Drink

Spanish cuisine is heavily influenced by a Moorish past. Staple dishes include the rice dish, Paella, Jamon Serrano (or Spanish ham), Gazpacho (cold tomato-based vegetable soup), roast suckling pig, chorizo (spicy sausage) and the Spanish omelette. Tapas (hot or cold snacks) are served with drinks in Spanish bars.

The most quintessentially Spanish drink is sangria, but a popular alternative with the locals is tinto de verano, or summer wine, a mix of red wine and lemonade. Vino Tinto or red wine compliments most meal choices. The preferred red grape type is Tempranillo, for which the regions of Roija and Ribera del Duero are famous. A well-known sparkling wine, Cava, is grown in Catalonia. Do try the Rebujito, a Seville style mix of sherry, sparkling water and mint. The most popular local beers are Cruzcampo, Alhambra and Estrello Damm. Coffee is also popular with Spaniards, who prefer Café con leche (espresso with milk).

Websites

http://www.idealspain.com

A detailed resource that includes legal information for anyone planning a longer stay or residency in Spain.

http://spainattractions.es/

http://www.tourspain.org/

http://spainguides.com/

http://www.travelinginspain.com/

http://wikitravel.org/en/Spain

Printed in Great Britain
by Amazon

35098667R00045